Under the Mango Tree

UNDER THE
MANGO TREE

FROM BLOOD DIAMONDS
TO BLOOD BROTHERS

BAMBAY SAWANEH
WITH LARRY REEVES

Xulon Press

Xulon Press
2301 Lucien Way #415
Maitland, FL 32751
407.339.4217
www.xulonpress.com

Scripture quotations taken from the New King James Version (NKJV).
Copyright © 1982 by Thomas Nelson, Inc. Used by permission. All
rights reserved.

Printed in the United States of America.

ISBN-13: 9781545625040

CONTENTS

DEDICATION ix

ACKNOWLEDGEMENTS .xi

MAP xii

FOREWORD xiii

CHAPTER 1: A MANGO SEED GROWS 1

CHAPTER 2: FAMILY STRUGGLES 7

CHAPTER 3: FROM MANGO TO DIAMONDS 11

CHAPTER 4: THE REBELS ARE COMING 17

CHAPTER 5: DISASTER UNDER THE MANGO . . . 21

CHAPTER 6: SISTERS OF HOPE 29

CHAPTER 7: MUSLIMS AT MANGO 55

CHAPTER 8: FOOTBALL BLESSINGS 59

CHAPTER 9: RETURN TO THE BEGINNING 67

CHAPTER 10: GREAT LESSONS LEARNED 71

DEDICATION

This book is dedicated to my wife, Mary, and to my family members who suffered with me through the terrible civil war in Sierra Leone.

ACKNOWLEDGEMENTS

S ister Ann Stevens who came to pray for me at my lowest point and then welcomed me into her home where she provided excellent care and encouragement.

Bill Turkovich who shared the gospel of Jesus Christ with me at a time when I was searching for answers and then provided support for me to enter Bible school to complete my education.

Mark Stewart who saw potential in me for ministry and provided support and a job with Hope Universal in Sierra Leone.

Joe Bacher who encouraged me to use my training in evangelism to minister to our community.

Samuel Menyongar who served as my mentor during the early days with Hope Universal.

Eric Baker who recognized my great joy and involvement in football and worked to help develop teams in Freetown and Makeni that became known as FC Seattle Sierra Leone.

David Fant who had a great passion for us to build a church at Mahawa where my hands are buried and has encouraged many in the USA to join in this ministry.

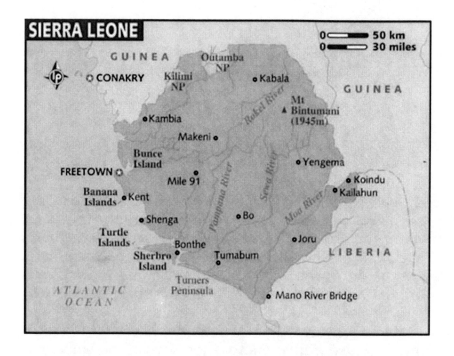

The map highlights two key locations in my story. Mahawa is a village near Makeni where the rebels attacked and destroyed family, friends and property and Kono is the diamond producing area of Sierra Leone near the Liberian border at Koindu.

FOREWORD

O n January 9, 2005, a team from South Carolina along with Mark Stewart from Seattle, traveled to Sierra Leone, West Africa, to conduct free medical clinics, to help with construction of a church and school, and to conduct conferences with leaders of Christian churches. For the next two weeks we stayed at the Javouhey House, which is located on top of a mountain overlooking Freetown, the capital of Sierra Leone. The Javouhey House is a Catholic guest house built in the late 1800s with a high wall for security and a beautiful view of the Freetown Bay. Living there was a young man named Bambay Sawaneh, who had no hands but a great smile and friendly attitude. Mark had met Bambay during his time as a missionary in Sierra Leone and was familiar with the story of how Bambay lost both hands during the terrible civil war which lasted from 1991 to 2002. There was agreement that Bambay's story should be shared with others who may be discouraged or think there is no hope for their future.

During recent conversations, Bambay revealed that some of the major events of his life happened under a mango tree. He was asked to provide a list of those events in order to develop the story of his life. This book illustrates the total depravity of man and the tremendous grace of God. It will make you cry and it will make you shout. At the end, you will be amazed at how the Lord can take a young man with no hands and bless hundreds of people.

Larry Reeves

I first met Brother Bambay Sawaneh at the Jahovey House in 1997 along with Bill Turkovich who I worked with from 1997 to 2001, a man that loves missions. Bambay was very shy and withdrawn. It was through Hope Universal Sierra Leone that I had the opportunity to disciple him as one of the team members and we travelled with him to the Republic of Guinea in 2005 and encouraged him to share his testimony at one of the churches where I was invited to speak. We also worked together at the Konde Farm Church and in the Hope Bible School. Over the years, Bambay has grown spiritually and we are so grateful to God that he is a leader in his community and an inspiration to many. His book will be a great encouragement to many who want to give up in life due to difficult situations that they may have gone through or are going through.

Samuel David Menyongar
President, International Missionary Center
Africa Center for Missions & Leadership, West Africa

CHAPTER ONE

A MANGO SEED GROWS

My name is Bambay Sawaneh of Mahawa village, Gbendembu Chiefdom, Boboli District, northern region of Sierra Leone, West Africa. I am the offspring of Amadu Sawaneh. My father was an Imam and very active in the Muslim religion. My mother's name is Yawolo Sawaneh. Siblings include Mohamed, Abu, James, Alpha, Kjadiatu, Kadiatu, Yawa, Esther Koroma, Kaday Koroma, and Isatu Sesay. I was born December 26, 1983, in the village Mahawa.

At one and a half years, my parents left the village to settle in Freetown, the capital of Sierra Leone. Freetown was a large city with many vehicles and small shops selling everything from clothes to food and even some new electronic items such as cell phones and CDs. The competition was strong and there was much shouting and accusing each other of cheating, but somehow they were able to have great verbal battles and then walk away as friends. Once in a while the arguments would get out of control and the police would come to break up the fights. There were two distinct issues causing fights. The first was the various language dialects resulting in the inability for folks to talk through their disagreements. The other issue was the natural quick temper of our people, which has been passed down for generations. Some people can stir up a fight by saying good morning in the wrong way. Coming from the farm out in the provinces, I was not accustomed to this type of verbal conflict. To a young child this was a frightening time. After a few years, I started school. There were no public schools, so my family had to pay the annual fees so that I could attend school. My father soon had a stomach problem which was said to be "not natural." Because of the deteriorating health condition of my father, we were forced to return to the village for traditional help. Back in the village, we continued farming. I was again sent to school. At this time, I was in class one. During those days, class level in pre-school was determined by your physical stature. Your hand, either right or left, should be able to go around your head and touch your ear. I was doing well in school but unfortunately my father's health grew worse and he could not afford to pay my school fees, so I had to drop out of school before I ended my first year. Father was taken to the nearby village called Ngugbaehun to a traditional healer, better known today as a witch doctor, where he stayed until he died very soon after moving.

Due to the many struggles in our daily family life, I was sent to live with my grandmother. At the age of five years my grandmother took me to church at a village called Kortuhun. Grandmother was the only Christian in our family, the others were Muslims. On the way coming back from church we met the cattle drivers traveling with their cows and they were eating mangoes and throwing away the seeds. I picked up one of the mango seeds and quickly put it in my pocket.

Grandmother asked, "What are you doing with that?"

2

I said, "I am going to plant it."

She told me to throw it away, but I refused and kept it in my pocket. She

beat me saying that I had soiled my trousers, but I insisted and took it home. When we arrived home, I took out my nablu (navel) and planted it with the mango seed. In our tradition, when a child is born the parents cut off the nablu and keep it until the child is full grown and matured, then they will give him or her that nablu. Since my father and mother were separated due to his illness, and I was sent to live with grandmother, I was quickly developing an interest in making things grow and serving others. I thought the nablu would make good fertilizer, so it was planted with the mango seed. That mango grew big and produced excellent fruit. It was called the Bambay Mango since we didn't know its name, like we know the names of other mangoes. The Bambay Mango became a blessing to our family and the village. Children played in the tree and neighbours would sit under the tree and talk about the crops, weather and their families for hours. The mango tree became the focal point of our village.

Before my mango tree started to produce fruit, my uncle used to take me to wash behind the burial ground where there was a nice pool of water and a great mango tree known as "the Dead Man's Mango." The fruit of that tree was outstanding, but not many people ate its fruit due to the location by the burial ground. The belief was that the mangoes grew large and sweet due to the blood from those who were buried in that graveyard. I really did not believe that old story and even if I did believe the story, I would have still eaten those mangoes since they were so good. It happened that every time they told me to go and wash, I would wait for my uncle because my uncle normally would go to the garden pool to wash, and going to the garden we had to pass through that burial ground and I could pick some mangoes to eat. Those good mangoes were helping me to wash frequently.

As I grew and learned more about farming, I would dream about a future date when I could have my own farm and provide food for many needy people. Since I attended a Christian church with my grandmother and all my other family members were Muslims, I was called a Chrismus. At that time there was no conflict between Christians and Muslims in our village, but the Muslims were the majority group and controlled most of the political offices in the national government and most village leaders were made up of relatives of the Muslim Chief who ruled and controlled the land. Sierra Leone had been a British colony until 1961 when the country was given independence from Great Britain. The British divided the land by issuing deeds to families, mostly farmers, who had lived there for many years. The family head became the community Chief over the land his family received. Even though the British had evangelized much of Sierra Leone, the majority were Muslims who became Chiefs and sometimes Imams. Mosques were located in every city and most villages. A few churches were built as a result of Catholic and Protestant missionaries during colonial days.

A wide range of economic status had developed from the extremely poor to the very rich with no middle class. The British had installed a rail system, hydroelectric generation site, and some well-constructed buildings in a few larger cities, but the areas outside the cities were basically villages with no water or electricity or sewage disposal systems. The diamond mines were operated by outsiders, primarily Lebanese, who owned the businesses and were making a good living while the local natives worked for them and barely survived. Some Sierra Leoneans had also developed farms and businesses which had allowed them to move to the upper class of society. When the British left, the country was without strong leadership and very little training to operate the infrastructure of railroad and power generation. The diamond mines were controlled by the government with those close to the leaders receiving most of the benefits, while the majority suffered in poverty. This combination of corruption and need was causing a growing discontent.

Living on the farm and working, our family was able to provide food and shelter but not much more. We did not consider ourselves poor but we really had no local rich people for comparison, so we were happy with our family and friends. Children were taught to obey their parents and work hard every day to help provide food for the family. The family was the focal point for children growing up. All activities, work and entertainment were done with the family. Since my father was no longer in the home, I had to begin to take leadership in the home and the village as a teenager. This was a difficult time, but looking back, I see that God was developing qualities that would benefit me and others in the future.

CHAPTER TWO

FAMILY STRUGGLES

B ack in the little village of Mahawa, I continued
working on the farm and helping my mother since
my father was now too weak to work. After a while my
father and mother were having constant conflicts. I
thought that it was due to his sickness, but I never
really understood. Finally, father left and went to a
near-by village hoping to get medical help.

During this time mother met a village man who
showed great interest in helping her with the farm.
He would come every day and do the heavy work of
planting and harvesting the crops. As a child, I did not
see any issues with this relationship and was thankful
to have him helping with the work that I was doing, in
addition to his kindness to my mother who was trying
to maintain the farm in my father's absence. As time
went on, others could see that our helper had more
interest than just being helpful during our time of need.

Mother divorced my father for the man who had
been helping us, which eventually led to the death of
my father. Since we were poor farmers and I was the

oldest child, my mother and step-father thought it best for me to live with my grandmother, as they started a new life in his home village of Shaun. At this time, I was left with my maternal grandmother who took me to Freetown to stay with an aunt in order to help me go school, but she too didn't have the means to send me to school, so I had to return to the village which became my home at grandmother's house.

After the death of my father and the remarriage of my mother, my paternal uncle, Foday Sawaneh, who had a son, requested that I live with him. Relatives of my father and mother agreed that this would be good for me since they thought my uncle would send me to school with his son. Instead, he took me to a farm to work for the next year. My uncle was an Imam, a trader and a farmer. He saw me as a means to increase his income by providing free labor. I would work on the farm and then help to carry the produce from the farm to market. One day as we were returning from a trade, we passed through the village where my mother lived with my step-father. When she saw me carrying a load for my uncle, she became very upset that I was not in school and that my uncle was taking advantage of me. A few weeks later she came and took me to her home at the village of Shaun.

At Shaun, my mother and step-father were farming but mother preferred having me work for her rather than for my uncle. So, I was again doing farm work and learning how to make things grow. We joined a coop-erative work team known as "ndorgor" in our dialect. After a year of work on the farm, my father's kinsmen came and took me away on the grounds that I should not stay with the man who caused my mother and father to separate, resulting in the death of my father.

This move to my father's relatives became a great challenge as I was becoming a teenager and no one was willing to take responsibility for my behaviour, so

I was free to roam from one place to another and living on food offered by those for whom I did menial jobs. During this time, I became seriously ill with no one to help. My mother heard I was sick and brought me home where she and her husband helped me to recover.

After that I asked my mother to allow me to learn a skill. She consented and sent me to another uncle, Komboh Sesay, who was a blacksmith. I worked as an apprentice for him three years. The work was difficult, but I knew it would provide opportunities in the days to come since Sierra Leone was growing and required more skilled workers. The tradition required that a graduate bring his parents to celebrate and say thanks to the teacher for his work and for the apprentice to receive a blessing, which would result in prosperity in that discipline. My parents were poor farmers and could not afford to take time away from their work to complete this rite, so my uncle and boss allowed me to return home to prepare for this ceremony. For the next year I worked on the farm and tried to save enough money to complete the blacksmith certification. After harvest, I was discouraged since I had not been able to save enough Leones to pay for the blacksmith graduation ceremony, so, I left home and went to Kono to work in the diamond mines, hoping to earn more than I could on the farm. As a young teenager, this was a big step of faith and at this time my faith was based only in myself, so I travelled with fear and wonder as to what I would find at Kono.

CHAPTER THREE

FROM MANGOES TO DIAMONDS

After moving to Kono and beginning work at the diamond mines, life seemed to be rather normal. The work hours were long but the pay was better than farming and many friends who had come to improve their income were working together during the week and playing football on weekends. We enjoyed some great games and always drew big crowds when we played in the lot near the diamond mine. After a few months, things started to change. The news was that Liberian rebels, led by Charles Taylor, had crossed into Sierra Leone and that some of the Sierra Leoneans, who were upset with the problems of governmental corruption, were joining the rebellion. A vigilante group of local citizens, called Kamajors, had formed to help defend their farms from the rebels and renegade soldiers. These folks were mostly farmers who had no military training and very few crude weapons but great courage and determination to challenge the rebels.

One day our village at Tankoro was attacked by the Kamajors who thought that we were rebels. Under heavy fire, the workers and their families ran for their lives out of the village. As the village people stampeded, my good friend Manso fell and was trampled to death by the crowd. Unfortunately, the regular soldiers of Sierra Leone were coming to Kono on the same trail as we were leaving, and they thought we were Kamajors. The trail was blocked and we were receiving fire from the soldiers, so we retreated back to Tankoro where we had no food. Since I had a little money, my friend Biamba Kapilego and I were encouraged to try to find food. As we travelled down the deserted path, we were stopped by a group of soldiers who accused me of being a Kamajor because I was wearing a native bib which they attributed to the militia fighters who were against them.

The spokesman for the group said, "Kill them."

At this point my friend, Biamba, escaped and ran home where he reported that I had been killed. The soldiers started beating me with their guns and sticks until I was nearly unconscious. Then another soldier arrived who appeared to be a senior officer and he asked, "Why are you beating him?"

They answered, "Because he is a Kamajor."

The senior officer said, "He is not a Kamajor, he is a diamond worker."

Then the officer said that he recognized me because, as he was passing through Tankoro, he had requested water and that I was the one who gave him a drink. Therefore, he was sure that I was not a Kamajor. After securing my release from the soldiers, the officer accompanied me through all the checkpoints and took me almost home.

That same day we received news that Akim had come and cleared the main road leading to Makeni. Akim was a very brave and fearless fighter who was considered patriotic and always fought in the interest of the people. It was believed that he possessed supernatural powers that made him invisible and bullet proof. So that night, together with thousands of people, we left Kono on foot for Makeni. Kono is about 150 kilometers from Makeni. At that time there were no vehicles on the roads in the whole country. So, we walked for over seven days and nights to get to Makeni without food. On our way we ate wild leaves and anything that would keep us alive and going. We left everything we had. Even the few things we brought along with us were dropped on the way because of the distance we had to cover. The journey was so long that even our shoes were abandoned on the way. Our feet got swollen and so it became very painful to walk. In the evening we arrived in Makeni. At Makeni we discovered that there were very few civilians in the city and the few we met were relatives of the soldiers and militias that occupied the city. It was like a ghost town with only soldiers and few civilians who were confined in specific areas. It was a frightening scene for every one of us but, with no available option, we had to stop over and spend the night there because we were so tired and needed rest. The following day I left Makeni for my village as everyone who came along with us from Kono was heading in different directions.

On my way, just about one and a half miles from Makeni, I saw from a distance a truck full of men in military fatigue approaching. I was afraid and tried to run but was unable because my feet were swollen. They stopped their vehicle, caught me and asked why I tried to run. I explained to them my ordeal and begged them not to kill me. They disclosed to me that they were government soldiers and assured me that they were not going to kill me. They asked me where I was going and I told them I was going to Mahawa, my mother's village and they told me that they were heading in the same direction and offered to take me in their vehicle. With apprehension and fear, I initially rejected their offer. After much encouragement, they assured my security and pleaded with me to join them, which I eventually did. They dropped me at Gbendembu, eight miles from my destination. During my journey with them, I was in a state of panic and dreadful fear that did not cease until we arrived at Gbendembu. Of course, the fear could be seen on my face. When I got down the soldiers could see the relief expressed on my face. So, they responded to my thanks with an outburst of laughter as they drove away.

From Gbendembu to Mahawa is eight miles. It was a tiresome, painful and restraining journey. I went slowly from one village after the other. Everyone in the villages I passed to my destination knew me and at sight they pitied and cried for me and some even offered me something to eat. It was real difficult for me to eat due to the blister in my mouth and throat as a result of many days without food.

Before I could get home, the news had already reached my mother and other relatives that I was on my way and in very bad shape. The entire village waited for my arrival and my mother had gone ahead to prepare food for me to eat. Finally, I arrived at Mahawa at about 4:00 p.m. and was received by my parents and friends with tears of grief. Almost everyone who knew me was crying for me, and I also could not hold my tears but joined the cry. I ate the food my mother prepared for me and afterward they also prepared some native medicine which they rubbed on me to help the swelling come down. After all this I went to bed and had a very sound sleep. It took some time for me to recover from the pain I sustained but after few months, I was up again and running.

The time I returned was harvest season, so I joined my mother again at the farm. It was during that period that we heard that the rebels and the renegade soldiers had been forced to retreat from Freetown and were scattered across the country doing great mayhem. Not too long afterward we heard that they were in our area. News of their attacks was getting closer and everyone was in panic. At this time, they were trying to regroup, yet people ran into hiding as rumors of their approach increased. We hid our belongings because we knew that they would spare nothing and that they were burning all property. There was no more cooking on an open fire in the village. Everyone had a hiding place in the bush where almost everything was done. While in the bush we heard that they had attacked Carina, a nearby village, and killed many people, amputated others, burned houses, looted properties and raped women. We were even told that they split open a pregnant woman's stomach, and drank the blood of the baby. Carina is about fifteen miles from my village, so we had to move from where we were, deep into the bush for safety. Soon the rebels came closer to our village and made their base there. At this time, we heard that the only medical practitioner within the whole area, who used to help people, had been captured and killed together with others. His name is Mr. Geyeba and he used to travel by bicycle across our villages, providing medical services to people. I am not sure he was really a medical doctor but he was a very good medical practitioner who was loved and was highly appreciated by the people. The news of the death of that man really triggered an exodus, so we moved further away.

The rebels had now regrouped and were in a very large number. All the villages had been deserted. They would raid one village after another and when they couldn't find anyone, they would loot everything. News of their atrocity reached the peacekeeping force that was based at Kalangba and they launched an attack on their position but could not overpower them, so they retreated to their base. It was after this that they became more dangerous and vicious. They went on the rampage, attacking and burning down every village they reached. In fact, all the civilians they captured who had been with them were executed. They were now so desperate and ruthless that they would climb high trees to watch for smoke. Anywhere they could see smoke they would attack and kill people, so people no longer would cook in the day. They would wait until night.

When the rebels could no longer see any smoke, they would resort to shouting test names, hoping that someone who bore a similar name in hiding would answer, thereby locating their position and then they would attack. We were now miles away deep in the forest. We used to sleep in the cover of big mango trees and in caves. No one trusted his fellow anymore and everyone was fighting now for survival. During this period of movement from one place to the other in the bush, my mother was pregnant and it was there that she gave birth to a baby boy who was named Alasan.

We had now been in the bush for over three months and had run out of everything. We lived on wild leaves and fruits. We would travel long in the night in search of anything that was edible. My mother had three little children, including Alasan, who because of the harsh conditions was becoming very weak and did not survive, but died there in the bush.

CHAPTER FOUR

THE REBELS ARE COMING

O n the 23rd of March 1991, a group of armed men who later were identified as the Revolutionary United Front (RUF) attacked a border town in the Kailahun district of the Republic of Sierra Leone called Bumara. This group, with support from the Special Forces of Charles Taylor's National Patriotic Front of Liberia, had just launched an insurgency that was going to devastate, ravage and completely wreck Sierra Leone in the years that followed. It was a rebellion that was going to claim the lives of over 50,000, mostly innocent Sierra Leoneans, and injured thousands of others, of which I am one.

"More than twenty years of poor governance, poverty, corruption and oppression created the circumstances for the rise of the RUF, as ordinary people yearned for change. These are the reasons why we started the war," claimed Foday S. Sankoh, who was the leader of the rebellion.

The first year of the war saw RUF taking portions of territory in the east and south of the country. As a result of the Liberian Civil War which started about fifteen months earlier, over 80,000 refugees fled from neighbouring Liberia to the Sierra Leone/Liberian border. This displaced population would prove to be an invaluable asset to the invading rebel armies because the camps that hosted these refugees, populated first by displaced Liberians and later by Sierra Leoneans, helped provide the manpower for the RUF's insurgency. The RUF took advantage of the refugees who were abandoned, starving, and in dire need of medical attention, by promising to provide food, shelter, and medical care. The government response to the insurrection was inadequate, morale in the military was low and the situation in the country was deteriorating fast. It was at this point that a group of young soldiers led by a 27-year-old captain, Valentine E. M. Strasser, staged a coup that deposed the A.P.C led government headed by a retired major general Joseph Siadu Momoh. The group that staged this coup was named National Provisional Ruling Council (NPRC). This was in 1992, barely a year after the rebel insurgency.

This turn of events brought a dramatic and radical change to the war. The new military government engaged the rebels in an all-out war and in the space of one year they succeeded in pushing the RUF rebels to the borders of Liberia. During the first year of the war, the RUF took control of territory in eastern and southern Sierra Leone, which were rich in diamonds. The government's ineffective response to the RUF, and the disruption in government diamond production, precipitated a military coup in April 1992 by the NPRC. By the end of 1993, the Sierra Leone Army (SLA) had succeeded in pushing the RUF rebels back to the Liberian border, but the RUF recovered and fighting continued. In March 1995, Executive Outcomes (EO), a South African based private military company, was hired to repel the RUF. Sierra Leone installed an elected civilian government in March 1996, and the retreating RUF signed the Abidjan Peace Accord. Under UN pressure, the government terminated its contract with EO before the accord could be implemented, and hostilities recommenced. In May 1997 a group of disgruntled SLA officers staged a coup and established the Armed Forces Revolutionary Council (AFRC) as the new government of Sierra Leone. The RUF joined with the AFRC to capture Freetown with little resistance. The new government, led by Johnny Paul Koroma, declared the war over. A wave of looting, rape, and murder followed the announcement. Reflecting international dismay at the overturning of the civilian government, ECOMOG forces intervened and retook Freetown on behalf of the government, but they found the outlying regions more difficult to pacify.

Since we lived in a remote village, the rebels had not reached our area but we had heard reports of their cruel actions in the areas around Freetown and Kono, the diamond district. One report was that the rebels had cut off the hands of men and young boys and that they had cut the stomachs of pregnant women and removed the babies and drank their blood. These actions were thought to give them strength and to intimidate their enemies. All the village people were afraid that at some point the rebels, who were being driven from Freetown, would come to our area. We were unarmed and helpless to confront a wild, usually drugged and ruthless army. Each day was spent in fear.

In May 1998, we ran from the rebels as they approached our village, going toward a village called Mahai. We then ran into the bush where there was a big mango tree that we hid under. My whole family and other families as well met under the mango tree in fear and trembling as we heard the sounds of gunshots and crying coming from the nearby village. This was the beginning of the rainy season and the thick branches of the mango tree provided some protection from the heavy rain. It was that mango and other mangoes around it that we depended on for food, but those mangoes were not enough for everyone and the children were crying. There was fear that the crying babies would attract the rebels, so my mother sent me to the village to check if people were still there and to come and tell her if some food was available for the children.

So, I walked by leg from the mango tree where we were hidden to the next village where I was sent, about 26 miles. On the way, I met some people in a village called Lohindie, including the town Chief who said we should go together to Mahawa village to collect some food. It is about 4 miles from Lohindie village to Mahawa village. I decided to go there and check on an old story teller called Pa Fondorwah. He was a blind man who lived at the back of my uncle Pa Samba's house.

When I knocked, he said, "Come and kill me." He thought it was the rebels.

I said, "It is me, Bambay."

Then he said, "Bambay, I need to eat and drink."

He had been left behind when the other village people ran from the rebels and, since he was old and blind, he could not follow them. I went to the other room and got water for him to drink and I went out and got him some big cherry mangoes from the tree near his house and he blessed me. He said he was expecting to die when all the village people ran but he was very thankful that I had returned to help him. He was around 89 years of age and probably would have died soon if we had not come. The mangoes were a great blessing to him.

CHAPTER FIVE

DISASTER UNDER THE MANGO TREE

―――――――❖―――――――

After gathering a supply of food, I was ready to return to my family in the bush under the mango tree. My uncle, Pa Samba, insisted that I sleep there since it was almost dark. He said it would not be safe for me to return during the night, since that was when the rebels usually attacked and we knew they were nearby. I was sleeping in the same room as my uncle and some other folks when there was a loud noise outside.

The rebels had reached our village and were killing our neighbours and burning their homes. I could hear women and children crying and men trying to reason with the rebels. Many of the rebels were young men who had been forced to join to save their own lives and now were heavily influenced by drugs to the extent that some of them had killed their own family members. It was almost as if they were demon possessed and uncontrollable.

Suddenly, there was a knock at the door of my uncle's house. We all lay as quietly as possible, hoping that they would go away. The rebels continued to knock harder and were cursing and yelling as they knocked. The makeshift door was made of palm thatch, weaved and placed at the entrance as a door with a rope in which a stick was passed from the inside. We had been asleep and in a brief moment I had a dream in which I saw the rebels in combat uniform scattered all around. Just then I realized the weaved-palm thatch door was over us. My uncle also got up thinking that a wind or something had pushed the palm thatch door and so he reached out for the stick that was behind the door and pulled it around. Since the door and its support structure were relatively weak, the rebels knocked the door down and came storming into the little dwelling. Some family members were able to run out the back and escape; some were butchered right there at the house. Many in the village were slaughtered as there was no one who was able to restrain the rebels.

Suddenly a very bright light was beamed on us and a voice shouted,

"They are here!"

Before we could make sense of what was happening, they had already descended with great violence and aggression. Immediately we were placed under gun point and were bundled out with our feet in the air. Right then they started beating and torturing with brutality and madness that people were treated worse than animals in the bush. Everyone in the village was rounded up. There was yelling and weeping everywhere. It was like hell descending. In a moment of time we were all gathered together in the center of the village. It was at this time that someone, presumably wanting to rescue me, approached me in the middle of the crowd and asked me to go and buy cigarettes for him. In a trembling voice I told him that there was no cigarette seller around the village. He insisted I go to the next village. As I was about to make my way through the crowd, they picked me out as a civilian, since all of them were armed. They shouted that a civilian was about to run away, so they quickly formed two parallel straight lines with all of them fully armed with all kinds of crude weapons.

Then someone said, "Pass through if you really want to go."

It was obvious they wanted to cut me into pieces had I made the attempt to pass through them, so I refused to try to run through the murder line. They then led me outside and began to accuse me of being their enemy.

One rebel said, "He is a Kamajor."

I said, "No, I am a farmer."

They apprehended me immediately and took me to their commander. When I was brought before him, he instructed them to prepare a letter for the President and then they placed the letter in a cassette, put it in my pocket, and told me to carry it to him. After that we were separated and all the old people were taken to a different location where they began to accuse us all of being Kamajors. We vehemently denied this accusation and then they accused us of being Civil Defense Force (CDF), which we also denied. They even said we were ECOMOG but we told them that we were farmers. So, they asked us to show our palms for inspection. According to them, they could detect by looking at our palms if we had ever handled and used a gun. After the inspection they concluded we were not fighters but farmers. Then they asked us for the money we had and we told them that we didn't have money and that we were poor farmers, who were only doing farming as a means of survival. They accused us again of being the ones that voted for President Ammed Tejan Kabba, who was the current President of Sierra Leone and thereafter threatened to kill all of us. So, we started begging. I even tried to let them know that I had not even reached voting age. For this they slapped me on my ear in a manner that I thought my ear would drop off. Each time I made an attempt to beg, they would hit me with an iron rod on my feet.

Later, we came to know why they separated the old people from us. They went to the old people and deceived them to believe that they were ECOMOG and that they had come to protect them. The older people believed their ploy and began to say bad things about the rebels. By the time they knew it was a ploy, it was too late. So, they came and reported to the commander all that the old people had said about them, so the commander ordered the operation to start. No one really knew what he meant by "Let the operation start" but everyone knew danger was imminent. People started crying and begging the commander for mercy but the cry and plea was of no avail.

The operation was about to start and the team was divided into three groups. The first group was responsible to interview, the second group was responsible to take prisoners behind the house, while the third group was responsible to maim and kill. The interviewer would display all types of guns and would ask if you had seen those kinds of guns with ECOMOG or the Kamajor. We were over thirty persons captured that night and we were asked to stand in a straight line and to move one after the other from the interviewer to the group behind the house. Behind the house was the massacre center. I was the second to the last person in line. One after the other the line descended as men walked like condemned prisoners on death row to their destruction. I can still hear the voices of screaming, yelling, crying and pleading. I can still hear the voice of men and women calling on God for help while I stood in the line waiting for my turn. As they cried behind the house for mercy, we cried in the line.

By this time, they had cut off the hands of my uncle and he lay dying on the ground with others who had been attacked. Blood was everywhere and the female sex slaves travelling with the rebels were complaining that the blood had sprayed on their clothes. I was taken outside under our mango tree and told to stretch out my arms. There was a large log under the tree where others had been forced to place their arms for amputation.

One of the rebels said, "Do you want long sleeves or short sleeves?"

I pulled back my arms and folded them close to my chest. Then two of the rebels grabbed me and tied my arms together and pulled them behind my back. They held my arms over the log and gave the order to cut. They had been using an axe to cut off hands of others and the axe was now dull, so, when they brought the axe down on my arms they were unable to cut all the way through. I was bleeding and the bones were crushed but part of the skin was still attached. Another rebel with a sharp machete came over and hit my remaining skin to totally sever the hands from my arms. The blood flowed and I was losing consciousness.

After destroying the village and killing or wounding the citizens, the rebels left us to die. Some of our neighbours who had been able to escape, came back and put cloths over our wounds as best they could. We all thought we would die before medical help could be found.

It was a scene of hopelessness and helplessness. Death stood straight before us and only God could save. Some died that day and others died later, but in the face of this hopelessness and helplessness I survived to tell this story. I cannot remember how they cut off my left hand and also cannot remember how they cut off the arm of the town Chief, Pa Ngaimoh, who was the last in line. In that state of unconsciousness, all of a sudden I heard the voice of someone shouting "Woo na don do me wok?" meaning "Have you finished my work?"

And then someone asked, "Who is that?"

He answered, "It is me, chamamraw" meaning chew it raw.

They told Chief Pa Ngaimoh that he was lucky because they are just about to finish and he had one hand left. At this moment I was getting a little conscious again of what was happening around me. The Commander came and asked chief Pa Ngaimoh to stand up. As he stood, blood from his newly amputated hand was spraying all over the place. In fact, the women, who had been captured and kept as sex slaves, complained again of the spray of blood but were immediately threatened to stop or they would turn on them. These women in very large number that I cannot quantify, of ages ranging from 12 to 25, were all tied up with armed men guarding them and any one of the rebels could sleep with them at will.

The Chief was commanded to pick up the piece of his right hand that had been cut off and eat it. Pa Ngaimoh resisted this command but, when beaten and tortured, he gave in and took his own hand and started eating it raw. After this incident they scattered away and left. They took with them some people including Fanta the daughter of chief Pa Ngaimoh and Hawa Sesay one of my cousins.

This was about 3:30 a.m. and in our pool of blood, we were left to languish and die. It was at this time that Chief Pa Ngaimoh started asking, loud enough for us to hear and in anguish and pain, if there was any one left alive. First it was my uncle Komboh who responded and through the assistance of the Chief, he got up and sat down and after a while I opened my eyes but could only see people very dimly. It was also difficult for me to get up because both hands had been cut off. Pa Ngaimoh again helped me and I got up. So, he went ahead to help everyone else to get up because he was the only one among us whose left hand was spared. Every one of us was weak and thirsty because of the considerable amount of blood we had lost. Chief Pa Ngaimoh encouraged us to move so we started our journey. It was a very painful one. The Rebels had taken away my belt from my waist, so as we set out, the trousers I was wearing came down. Since I had no hands anymore and due to the pain and the weakness, I just removed the trousers and left them behind. That was how I left the letter and cassette behind and I could find it no more.

As we went along, some fell and Pa Ngaimoh would help them up and encourage them to press on. At one point we came to a pond of water on the street and we had been very weak and thirsty and wanted to drink. Chief Ngaimoh fetched this dirty water and helped all to drink. On our way to Makeni village we met a group of people and from a distance started calling them to come and help us, but when they saw our condition, they ran away. Even when Chief Ngaimoh ran after them to beseech them to come to our aid, they still fled because of the gruesomeness of our sight. It was at this village that my brother Abu finally gave up on the journey; he was so weak that he could no longer go further and there we left him. Not too long after, Chief Ngaimoh decided that because he himself was now getting weak; he could not go ahead. It was at this moment that I also became so weak and then fainted and fell. Chief Ngaimoh no longer had the strength to help me up and so he left. Uncle Komboh left me, but from a short distance from where he left me, he too fainted and fell.

Chief had gone ahead and, according to him, on his way met three petty traders, Alimamy, Samuel and another guy whose name I cannot remember. These guys usually came to our village and the surrounding villages to do business. He told them that we were in a very bad condition and pleaded with them to go and help us. So, these traders, who had kept their goods in the bushes, came to our rescue. I had regained consciousness and was lying down on the street where Chief left me, when I saw three men from a distance coming toward me. Helpless and hopeless, I thought it was the rebels so I started shouting to them to come and finish me off. Upon hearing this, they started crying and told me that they were not rebels but are the petty traders who usually came to us in our village to do business. One of them picked me up on his back and another went also for Uncle Komboh and picked him up and on their backs and took us to a town called Kalangba, which is the headquarters of Gbendembu Ngowahun Chiefdom. It was also the base of ECOMOG and the pro-government local militia groups. The three traders that brought us to this base were so angry with all the troops that they demanded that they give them weapons to go and fight the rebels, since the troops were sitting down there and doing nothing to prevent the rebels from destroying their people. The troop commandeered a vehicle owned by one popular driver, commonly known as Musa, in our area and took us to Makeni.

CHAPTER SIX

SISTERS OF HOPE

F inally, after three days of walking and then covering the last few miles in Musa's vehicle, we reached Makeni where a hospital was still operating and the Catholic Nuns took us in, bandaged our wounds and provided food and water. For the first time in many days, I was beginning to have some hope of living through this sample of Hell on earth.

Upon arriving in Makeni, we were taken straight to the Makeni Government Hospital. The Chief Medical Officer of the hospital was Dr. Barker. Without any medical treatment, the doctor told us that there were no medical supplies and therefore he could do absolutely nothing to help us but, he said, "If anyone could afford to get the necessary medicines, he would do the operation."

At this time everyone was crying for us and suddenly one of the nurses volunteered to get me all the medicine needed for my operation. Her name was Tuzelene Virol John. She went and got the medicine for the operation. Immediately after that I was taken to the operation theatre where the doctor performed the operation successfully. After the operation, there was difficulty getting medicine to treat the wound. But the doctor would come around daily to clean up the wound even though there was no medication to apply.

On the third day of my being in the Makeni Government Hospital, they brought Abu, my uncle, who we left on the way but he was in a very bad condition, though he was still alive. He had been lying down in the village where we left him all this while and before they could get to him the wounds were already rotten and he was now in a terrible state. For the past three days since I had been brought to the hospital, I had not been able to sleep because of the pain. I would faint and go off frequently because I had lost so much blood and the hospital could help me but very little.

On the fourth day some Catholic sisters came to the hospital to pray for the sick. One of them, who I later knew as Sister Ann Stevens, came to my bed and prayed for me and after the prayer, she asked me about my parents. So, I explained the circumstances that landed me in the trouble. I told her that my mother did not even know about what had happened to me and that she is all the way in the forest in our area. She offered to take me home and help, provided I knew someone who would go along with us who knew the way she was to carry me. I told her that I knew no one there, but fortunately one of the nurses volunteered to go with us. We went together with the nurse to Sister Ann Stevens' place and there I saw other amputees who had been there receiving treatment. Immediately they gave me some treatment and eventually I fell asleep after many days. The medical treatment here was much better than what I had received in the hospital, so in a matter of days I was getting better. I began to get very good sleep, but in my sleep, I would see the rebels and would jump up from my sleep screaming.

This in turn made me afraid to sleep. When they discovered that I was unable to sleep they brought in an Italian doctor, Dr. Rita, who used to dispense an injection that helped me to sleep. I really cannot tell the type of drugs she used to dispense but one thing was sure, it helped me to sleep even though I still used to have the nightmare of the rebels.

While we were in the government hospital, on several occasions I asked the doctors to help provide for us any poisonous substance that would kill us, because we felt that it was not worth living anymore. Both hands were gone, there was no medicine in the hospital and we knew nothing about our family members. We were in severe and excruciating pain; the hope of life was all gone, so we opted for death with no fear.

One day I requested permission from Sister Ann to visit the government hospital where my uncles were still admitted. So, she assigned someone to accompany me to the hospital. At the hospital, I met my uncles but their conditions were not improving in any way. They lamented their pains and told me that mine was much better than theirs now and that this was the reason they were opting for death. We all started crying so, immediately the person that was accompanying me hurried me away back home to Sister Ann. That evening my Uncle Komboh Sesay committed suicide and died. He threw himself down the stairs and broke his neck and ended it all. As people started crying for the death of Uncle Komboh, my other Uncle Abu, who was lying in a hopeless condition, asked if it were one of his brothers that had died. He demanded to know specifically if it were the younger or the older one that had died. They told him no one was dead, trying to conceal the truth of what had happened. So that same night he too, Uncle Abu, passed away. Uncle Komboh and Uncle Abu were siblings from the same mother and father. They both died on the same day and were buried on the same day. I am the son of their sister. The news of the death of my two uncles came to me the following morning and it was devastating for me. They prevented me from going there with fear that I would collapse and die also.

News of the gruesome, barbaric, and savage attack on us had spread all around the region. The sight of this attack had been discovered and the amputated hands found. I used to wear a ring, which most people from our community knew belonged to me. I was known all around our community because I was a footballer and a blacksmith. Also, the trousers I left behind were known to belong to me, so with all this they quickly knew that I was involved in this attack. The survivors, who returned to Mahawa village, buried our hands under a large mound of earth which remains there to this day.

The news reached my mother in the bush that I had survived and was in the Makeni hospital. She quickly found her way to Kalangba where she got a vehicle to Makeni. At Makeni she went to the government hospital and was directed to Sister Ann's place where I was staying. When she saw me, she fell on the ground with tears, blaming herself for being responsible for what had happened to me, and with tears asking me to forgive her. At this sight I also joined her in the cry. The sisters came out and consoled us to stop the crying.

The Convent did not have a place for my mother to stay so she spent the day with me and left for Makeni, where she stayed and occasionally visited me. There were over fifty amputees staying in the Convent under the care of Sister Ann Stevens, a member of the Catholic Sisters of Cluny. The first operation done on my hand was not entirely complete as the bones still needed to be restored. Later Sister Ann took me for another operation which was done successfully. I had stayed at that time for almost one year in the Convent when one day Sister Ann informed us that she had heard of an operation done by the International Red Cross which could help us be able to do something for ourselves. The operation she said was known as Hook and Bug and she promised to take us to Freetown and, if we liked the operation, then it would be done. She took us to Freetown eventually and we were taken to Netland Hospital at Congo Cross in Freetown.

At Netland we were again given the details of the operation, which we initially were afraid to undertake because of fear of the pain, but the doctors educated us on the significance of the operation to our continuous livelihood and encouraged us to consent and undertake it, which we eventually did. On the night before the day of the operation, we were asked not to eat anything in preparation. The day of the operation eventually came and the procedure was carried out successfully. After the operation, I had to stay for some months for the healing and another four months for physiotherapy. After this we were discharged and returned to Makeni. On our way back, we met the rebels that had attacked and captured a major bridge that linked the northern Province to the capital city Freetown, called Gbairay Bridge. We had to spend almost two days before the government soldiers came and repelled them and provided escort for us to Makeni. We arrived in Makeni on Sunday and proceeded straight to the Convent, which had now turned into our new home. At the Convent again, they started an adult literacy education program for us as most of us amputees had never been to school and many more had dropped out of school early. This literacy class was really very helpful for most of us who wanted to improve our educational standard. Life in the Convent was getting interesting and really encouraging for almost all of us. The Catholic Sisters were always around to encourage and play with us. They would teach the word of God and pray with us. We had almost everything we really needed and that

helped us not to constantly remember the hopelessness of our condition.

One day as we were seated together with Sister Ann
and some other sisters, I told Sister Ann that I could
recognize the fellow who cut off my hands if I ever saw
him. She then asked me what would be my reaction
if I happened to see him. I told her rightly and bitterly
that I would love to kill him. Immediately she started
teaching me about forgiveness from the Bible and I
became angry with her for suggesting that nothing be
done to the man that had caused me so much pain
and permanent disability. But she was so patient and
courageous to continue together with the other sisters
in the Convent to teach me and others to forgive those
who had hurt us.

While in the Convent, the rebels attacked a village
called Binkolo about three miles from Makeni. Binkolo
is the home town of the deposed president of Sierra
Leone, Major General J.S Momoh. As a result of this
attack, the sisters had to be evacuated to Freetown
and we were given some money to find our way. It was
really a difficult moment for both the sisters and us,
but much more for the sisters. Nevertheless, they had
to go and leave us behind. They left that morning and
we left the Convent in the evening amidst heavy gunfire
close to the city of Makeni. We were heading back to the
village where we had left in a pool of blood. The village
where we were massacred and brutally butchered, the
village where our hands and limbs were chopped off.
This is the village we were forced to return to again. It
had been almost two years since I left this village and
almost two years since I was made permanently dis-
abled. There were no vehicles available at this time, so
we had to move on foot. It was a very difficult trip as we
had to travel using a by-pass route to avoid the rebels
as much as possible, trusting God alone to guide and
lead us safely. We arrived the following day at the village

where we had been attacked and amputated. The village was in ruins, with almost all the houses destroyed and the town covered with bushes. We reached the very spot where the incident took place and discovered that the people had covered the remains of our hands and limbs with a heap of dirt.

The memory of our brutal torture came back fresh to me and immediately I burst into tears. There were only a few people left in the village, so they came around me and joined me in the cry. Those in the bushes heard the noise of crying in the village and were afraid, mistaking it as another attack, but were later informed that it was one of the survivors of the brutal massacre that had returned. So, they came out and joined in the crying. They were in very bad shape with hairs grown like wild animals and they stood like skeletons. I was frightened with the state of their condition and straightway started thinking how I was I going to survive in such a place where even those with two hands were in such condition. It was a dreadful moment for me, thinking how I would manage to go about with them in the bush without hands. I asked them about my village, but they told me that they knew very little and according to them people did not move easily around at that time.

From there I continued the journey to my own village which is about three miles from the place of the gruesome incident. I arrived at my village and found no one there. Everyone had taken refuge in the bush. I had no alternative but to enter the bush in search of some one. On my search in the bush, I came in contact with one boy who was out in search of food. He told me that he knew where my uncle Samba Sesay and family were hiding in the bush and agreed to take me there. His one condition was that I had to go with him to his own hiding place and pass the night there and from there he would take me to my uncle because, according to him, the place where my uncle was hiding was far. I agreed and followed him and the following day, he took me to my uncle.

Upon our arrival he too and the entire family started crying when they saw me. After all the weeping and expressing of sorrow over me, I asked them about my mother. My uncle told me that he had heard that my mother came back from Makeni some time ago and was hiding somewhere in the mountains but he did not know the exact location. So, I stayed with him for over seven months in the bush without seeing my mother. Over this period, he made every effort to locate my mother, which he eventually did. He went for her and brought her and upon seeing me she started crying, which I also did. Our stay together was not too pleasant because she kept on crying, so I decided to leave her for Freetown.

There were no vehicles at that time, so it had to be by walking. Walking from where I was to Freetown was not really an easy thing but it was the only option if I needed to reach Freetown. I left using the by-pass route, as it used to be known, to Freetown. Two days after my departure, on my way I met others who were also going to Freetown and so I joined them. We would walk for the whole day and pass the night in any village that accepted us. We would talk to the town chief or whosoever we would meet in the town, requesting them to allow us to sleep there and would continue our journey very early the following day. At one point in our journey we arrived at a river where there was a militia checkpoint. They apprehended all my travelling mates and accused them of being rebels and resolved to kill them. I pleaded for their release but to no avail, so I ran to the previous village where we spent the night and pleaded with the town chief to come with me and talk to the militia not to kill them. The town chief accepted and eventually came with me. He pleaded with them and assured them that they were

36

not rebels but civilians who passed the night in his village last night. The militias listened to the town chief and released them. We crossed the river and continued our journey.

It took me eight days to arrive at Lungi. Lungi is the town that hosts the international airport and it is just a few miles to Freetown. I crossed over to Freetown in total confusion as to where in Freetown I would head since I really did not know any specific person in Freetown. In this state of confusion, I came across three of my old friends Patrick Musa, Santos Kallon and Alimamy Kanu. They asked me where I was staying and I told them that I was just arriving in town and did not have a place to stay, so they took me with them to their house at Kroo Bay, a slum community in the heart of the city on the Atlantic coast. Later on, I came to discover that they were just squatting in one small room which was not even theirs and was not spacious enough to accommodate everyone, so that night we stayed in the Community Mosque. Something real funny took place in the mosque the following morning. Early in the morning when the people came to offer their morning prayer, my friends got up and left without waking me. Due to the long journey I had just completed, I was real tired and was still sleeping. The people also did not bother to wake me up but went straight into their prayers. Almost at the end of their prayers there is a word that they will all recite together. It was the sound of that collective "Amen" that woke me up. I jumped up in panic and fled with speed out of the mosque. It was really a funny situation.

The following day we went out for a walk and during that walk I came in contact with one of my cousins called Finoh Koroma. He was so glad and shocked to see me because he had heard that I died in the hospital in Makeni. I explained my ordeals and told him that I just came in yesterday and the place I was squatting was not good. He told me that he did not have a place for himself but slept in the vehicle that he was serving as a conductor, but promised to take me to one Mr. Sorry, who he said he would plead for accommodation for me. So, I went along with him to Pa Sorry. He introduced me to Pa Sorry and made the request. Pa Sorry in response said that his place was too small and already full but that if I were ready to sleep in the parlour with other members of his family, he would have no problem. He offered to ask his wife to give me food anytime she cooks. I stayed with Pa Sorry, sleeping in a chair in his sitting room. While there, I started searching for the Catholic Sisters. Life started getting tougher for me because, with Pa Sorry, food was not always enough and it came always very late in the evening. I would starve for the whole day with nothing to eat. I would have to go to the ghetto to see if could get something to eat and sometime the guys at the ghetto would be helpful with whatever they had. As I became frequent there, they lured me into smoking marijuana. They convinced me that if I smoked I would forget my problems and enjoy life. I succumbed to their appeal and started smoking. The first day I smoked, I slept for almost the whole day and when I woke up I was so weak and nervous with a headache. I was also so hungry with nothing to eat. This continued for a while until I discovered that it was taking a toll on my health, so I decided to find another solution.

I told my cousin to take me to any camp that hosts amputees. He told me he knew of one at Aberdeen road and eventually took me there. We went there and met with the camp chairman called Mr. Gabriella. He told us that there was no space in the camp to accommodate me and advised us that life in that camp was really difficult because, according to him, even food is hard to get. He even informed us that there are so many who have come recently but there is no place at all for them. I asked if he knew of anywhere Catholic Sisters could be found. He informed me that he knew a place in Brookfield where I could find them. He directed us to the place and we left. The same day we went to the place where he directed us and fortunately I met Sister Ann Stevens there. She was so glad to receive us and immediately she gave me some money to go to the hospital because my physical condition was really bad with rashes all over my body. Besides the money, she also gave me things to wear. I continued to come to see Sister Ann at her Brookfield Convent and there met with other amputees. We started sharing our experiences and challenges with each other. As time went on we started facing accommodation difficulties so we shared it with Sister Ann who later rented a place for us at Congo Town. Five of us, all amputees, shared that single but spacious room. Sister Ann continued to work with us and helped us in many things. Again, she opened an adult literacy class for us and conducted several workshops to train us in various skills and disciplines to help us become self-reliant.

Life was really difficult. Our only source of help was the Catholic Sister who would give us five thousand Leones every Saturday, but that was far from being enough for a week. Sometimes our neighbours would offer us food, but it was too small for all of us. As things became more difficult especially with our daily food, one neighbour, Madam Fatmata Conday, seeing our struggle made an arrangement with a local restaurant to give us the craws and crumbs. That proved to be real helpful to us as it provided a daily source of food.

As things became more difficult, one day on our way to the adult education center, we noticed that someone was following us. Later we came to know him as Mr. Abdul. He met and told us of an asylum program in Guinea for Sierra Leonean refugees and offered to help us apply for it. Immediately, the five of us agreed to follow this man to Guinea. We left the following day at 3:00 p.m. by sea with a local boat called Pampa and travelled until we came close to Conakry but it was too late for the Guinean authority to allow us land, so we waited under very heavy rain till morning. In the morning we landed and followed Mr. Abdul home.

We were trying to obtain the asylum form when, one day on our way to UNHCR's office, we were rounded up by a community chief who told us that there was a coup d'état in Guinea and that they were pointing the finger at Sierra Leonean and Liberian refugees and had started arresting them, so he wanted to help protect us. We accepted his offer and went to his house where we met many other Sierra Leonean and Liberian refugees seated in his sitting room. Not too long after, we heard the sound of sirens coming toward our direction and before we knew it, an army truck was standing before the house and suddenly all of us were arrested and thrown into the truck. They took us to a location which I did not know and put us in an open hall where we met other Sierra Leoneans and Liberians. We spent about three days without food. Occasionally some people would bring pap and bread for us and the arresting authority would allow them give it to us. We were free on the third day and we went home. The following day I heard that the Sierra Leone government was sending a ferry to evacuate their nationals from Guinea. So, I decided that I should return home and face life. My reason was not far-fetched. I left home with the hope that life would get better for me but it had turned out to be exactly the opposite. I preferred going back home and suffering rather than suffering in another man's land. I joined the ferry headed back home. It was indeed a very interesting and difficult journey. There were thousands of Sierra Leoneans in Guinea at that time and almost everyone wanted to return. So, it was really a fight to secure a place on board the ferry. Graciously I entered the ferry and we set out for Freetown. It was almost a two-day's journey but we arrived in the early hours of the day, too late to allow us enter the queue. We waited till it was clear before we were finally permitted to land.

Upon my return, I went to see Sister Ann at her Convent in Brookfield. I explained to her my ordeals in Guinea. I even gave details of some of the difficulties I encountered and she responded by encouraging me not to give up but to be resilient and confident of the future. I was very clear about my lack of hope in view of the fact that I had no hands and therefore would not be able to do anything for myself anymore. In her encouragement, she asked me how many body parts I had. I started mentioning my body parts by name until I almost exhausted them. She then told me that I should not lose hope for just losing a part of my body. She let me know that there are many other parts still intact to help me succeed in life. Realizing that we were still traumatized, she conducted a week-long trauma healing awareness campaign for us. She employed the services of one Dr. Carew and Sister Betty to help us de-traumatize. This trauma healing counselling and training helped us change our perceptions and we began to look at ourselves differently than before. We began to regain our personal worth and eventually hope for the future. Sister Ann was very much concerned about how we could be self-reliant and independent of others for our livelihood, so she conducted a business training program for us. This program was facilitated by Grace and Antonia. After this, a man came from Canada called Mr. Quentin, who was working with Cause Canada. I really don't know how he met with Sister Ann, but one day sister Ann called us to meet Quentin. She told us of Quentin's desire to help us establish a small-scale business. In that meeting we were asked which kind of business we would like to do. After consultation with others, we told them we would like to sell used clothing (junks). He told us that he knew some guys who had been involved in the sale of used clothing and would consult him to inquire if it would be profitable and what type of used clothing that we could sell in the raining season, as it was in the rainy season then. He eventually met the fellows who we later knew as Rashid and Mohammed and was advised that it was profitable and also the type of clothes to sell. In the process, Quentin decided to visit our residence. On his visit, he discovered that there were so many things that we lacked and decided to help us get them. He bought for us one bag of rice, spoon, port and other home utensils we lacked. It was on this visit that we agreed on the date and time to meet Rashid and Mohammed to help us in the purchase of the used clothing. These guys had earlier advised on the type of clothing to buy so we needed them to guide in the process. We identified a spot somewhere around the central police station, just at the entrance of the road leading to the government wharf by a big market and Quentin helped us erect a structure for the sale of the used clothing.

With the help of Rashid and Mohamed, we all together with Quentin went to buy the goods. We started the sales the following day at the spot where we had built, but unfortunately for almost one week we only sold one item. Seeing the slowness of the sales, I decided to go around with items for sale in the city. It was still the same thing; business was slow. People told us that such goods are not for city dwellers but for those it the interior. We informed Quentin of the slowness of the sales and the advice of the people and he instructed us to reduce the price, which we did. We resolved to move the business to the Congo Market, were people usually go for cheap things, but this also did not yield any good result for we spent almost a week there and sold only two pieces. So, we reported back to Quentin who told us to gather everything together, which we did. He came and we audited it and everything was correct. He expressed his disappointment in the advice of Rashid and his friend and was really disheartened that the venture which he had expected to help us has now failed. He told us to wait patiently until he could talk to Sister Ann.

Later, Sister Ann called us and asked what else would we like to do? I told her that I would like to do farming as this was what I had learned from my parents. I further told her that I might not be able to do the type of rice farming I used to do but would do a vegetable garden and livestock farming. She informed me that such type of farming was done at Leicester village where she said they had farm land and asked me to go along with her to see the place. We went and I saw that the place which was indeed good for such venture.

Quentin again got me the necessary tools and seed I needed to start. It was a very difficult venture for a man who does not have two hands to be involved in such activity, but by the help of God I got a thought which helped me. There is a device which lame people, especially those who don't have hands, use to help them grip things and carry things. I now decided to tie the hoe to the device and then to my arm with the help of the driver of the Javouhey House called Mr. Karamu. This enabled me to dig holes and also make hills, but the rope that was used to tie the hoe to the device continued to be cut off due to the force that is used to dig, so I got another idea which was to nail the hoe to the device permanently and that proved real successful. I planted corn, eggplant, runner beans, lettuce, sweet pepper and potato leaves. The crops did so well that the manager of Javouhey House, Mrs. Victoria Conteh, admired the growth and even said that others who had planted on the farm had not gotten that kind of growth and she decided to look for a market for me.

She consulted the St. Joseph Convent Primary and Secondary School and they agreed to buy the produce. The first harvest was good and we supplied and were paid. The other subsequent harvests were bought by the Javouhey House and others. Because of the cost of production on the garden, Sister Ann thought it would be wise to try poultry. She shared it with me and I accepted it and with her help we set up a poultry farm. We started with a hundred chickens. But before this, Sister Ann had arranged with a poultry farmer, Pa Flood, for me to receive training on poultry management and care. I went there every day for over a month and practically learned how they operated their farm. After that I went to other farms to learn.

Through the training acquired I was able to manage my own poultry quiet well. One day as I was marketing the eggs of my poultry, I came in contact with Major Peter Golden of the International Military Advisory Teaching Team (IMATT) that was stationed around Leicester Peak Junction. When he saw the eggs, he was really fascinated and asked me the source of the eggs. I told him that it was a product of my poultry. A few days later he came jogging and met me and some other folks playing football around the area where my poultry was. I took advantage to show him my poultry. When he saw the chickens, and learned that they were my produce and saw that I did not have hands, he was really thrilled. He asked how I sustained the injury and when I explained how I got amputated, he was shocked in disbelief and almost wept. Moved with compassion he promised to tell his team about the poultry and that very evening, he invited me for a dinner at Family Kingdom.

The day following, he came with one of his friends called Major Mark to see the poultry. Major Mark also admired the enterprise and encouraged me to continue. They left and afterward made arrangements with their team to buy from me. One of the reasons they patronized my poultry was the proximity of the poultry to their camp. During this time, I used kerosene lanterns to power the poultry farm and this was very expensive. So Major Peter decided to help electrify the poultry which was a great contribution. Major Peter and Mark used to take me and my friends out to the beach to spend time with us and encourage us to be happy. They also used to give us footballs and other things to play which really made me happy.

One day, sometime in 2001, I was working in the garden digging and making some hills when I heard a voice behind me calling "brother, brother," and when I lifted up my head I saw a white man walking towards me. I had never seen him before and I was wondering what the matter was. He greeted me and I also returned the greeting. He introduced himself as Bill Turkovich, a missionary from International Missionary Center (IMC). He asked me for my name and I told him, "I am Bambay Sawaneh."

He asked me where I lived and I told him I lived in the compound and that I was the one planting the garden. He then told me that he had been watching me work for quite some time and that he had the impression that I was a hero and that is what had drawn him to me. I asked what he meant by the word hero, since I did not understand what he meant. So, he told me that a hero is a mighty warrior that everyone admires and respects. He then asked me,

"Who is the greatest fighter of renown and reputation in Sierra Leone?"

So, I said, "It is Akim."

Then he said, "That's who you are, you are even greater than Akim."

So, I was shocked and amazed and stood gazing at him in disbelief. He said that the reason he said that I was greater than Akim is that I would be a mighty fighter, but not with the physical weapon that Akim used to fight but that I would be a hero for Christ. He then told me that God wanted to use me. He started preaching to me about Jesus Christ. I told him that I was a Muslim, because my late father was an Imam and all other members of my family were Muslims. He then asked me if I had ever heard about Jesus Christ. I told him that the Catholic Sisters had told me about Jesus Christ, encouraged me with the Bible, and would always take me to church. He said that is fine, but he would like to continue to talk to me about Jesus Christ. I told him that I was already busy working, but he insisted, so I gave him ears.

He shared the gospel of salvation with me and with joy I accepted Jesus Christ as my Lord and Savior and he led me in prayers. Immediately after the prayers, he told me that he would love to send me to Bible school to study the word of God. In response I told him that I have not been to school enough to go to Bible school. He said that if only I were willing and available, God would make me capable. I consented to his offer and he asked me to go with him right then and there. I told him that I was working and besides I was dirty, so it had to be another time. He still insisted that I should come with him and asked me to just wash up and follow him. I reluctantly left my work and was on my way to wash up when he offered me Le 30,000 for the work I was leaving to follow him.

I washed up and joined him in his car and we left for Circular Road in Freetown. This address housed the office of International Missionary Center (IMC) down stairs and the Freetown Bible Training Center (FBTC) upstairs. Upon our arrival, he took me to the IMC office and introduced me to all the staff that were present and afterward took me upstairs to FBTC office. He greeted every one and proceeded to meet with the Director of the Bible School. After some time, he came out together with the Director and other staff members and they welcomed me and asked me to start school the following Saturday. They directed me to the campus that I was to attend as there were many campuses across the city. They also told me of the schedule and other related information. Bill took me back home and it was a very great day for me.

Saturday came and I was up and ready for school. This was my first day in Bible school. I dressed in a track suit and wore boots and here I was on my first day in FBTC. I arrived late that morning and proceeded to the administration office. The Administrator was Brother Ola Tunji. He welcomed me and asked for my name which I quickly gave him. He gave me my badge and asked one of the staff to accompany me to my class. When I arrived and entered the class, I quickly noticed that I was the only one without hands in the entire class and immediately I felt ashamed and a bit embarrassed, so I tried to hide my amputated hands in my pockets so that I might pretend to have hands. We came out for a lunch break and I still kept my hands in my pockets. People greeted me with outstretched arms but I would not respond. I was so ashamed that I found a place among the flowers in the compound and there I sat and wept. I cried as if I had just lost my hands.

As I was crying, the school Director, Rev. Donald Bestman, came along and found me crying bitterly. At first, he didn't know who I was, or my condition. He tried to inquire from me what the matter was, but still I could not open up and tell him anything. My hands appeared to be deep in my pockets. He tried to pick me up from the ground and in the process, he noticed that my two hands were missing. He then recognized me as the young man who came with Bill to his office and was very sad about my condition. With his hands on my back, he took me to his office and then he really encouraged me with the word of God. From that time,

I took courage and embraced myself with the determination that I would not allow my condition to intimidate me to leave the Bible School. I continued school and gradually I started understanding scriptures and my entire lessons.

Bill left a few weeks later but paid my school fees for a year and made an arrangement with Samuel Menyongar for my transport allowance. After my first year graduation, Bill was no longer around to help me pay my fees so I had to depend on the proceeds of my garden work to continue schooling.

One day I received information that World Hope International (WHI) had come with false hands and were distributing them to amputees, so I went there and got one and then I went for physiotherapy in Freetown. I entered the office and met a man sitting by the door. As I was making my way through, he drew my attention and greeted me and afterward he asked me where I was amputated. I turned to see who this person was and behold it was the very man who had amputated me. I ran out in tears to my friend Santos Kallon and told him that I had found the man who amputated me. I had always said to them that,

"If I ever see the person that amputated me, I will recognize him."

At that time Santos was drinking water from the tap but upon hearing that, he immediately stopped drinking and said,

"Let's go kill the man!"

At that instance I remembered the teachings I had receive from Sister Ann on forgiveness. Santos was still urging me to call other amputees to go after the fellow and kill him. We entered the hall but didn't find the man so we came out and found him standing by a tree around the building. I was still crying when Santos in anger approached him and asked him if he knew the guy who was crying over there, referring to me. He said no and asked Santos to call me. As I was approaching, he took a stick of cigarette and offered it to me. I rejected and told him I didn't smoke. He then offered me again five hundred Leones which I also rejected. At this point Santos asked for his name and he said he was Alimamy.

Santos further asked him, "Where do you come from?"

In response he said, "I am a Limba by tribe."

Then Santos asked, "Do you speak Limba?"

He said yes, so Santos spoke Limba to him, but he could not understand, with the excuse that he didn't stay long in his home town. He was asked what his mission at the office was and he said he came to visit his brother, Ibrahim, who was in charge of the physio-therapy. We called Ibrahim and asked him if knew him and if he were his brother. He stood still for a while but did not answer. At this point he ran away into the office building and shut the door.

All the amputees present ran after him, including others that were around the scene and those who had been victims of rebel atrocities, when they heard that a man that cut and amputated a young man had been caught. The people gathered demanding that the man be handed over to them or they would burn the building. But I, still crying, came forward and told the crowd that there was no need of killing the man since I had already forgiven him and that killing him would not bring my hands back and that I had left my case with God.

The whole crowd got angry with me and said that they had not forgiven him and would not forgive him because he was part of the group that killed their fathers, mothers, sisters and other relatives and ampu-tated their brothers, burned their houses and were responsible for their sufferings. So, I continued to plead for them to forgive him and let him go. In the process, someone in the office, after identifying him, said that he was the one who almost drowned him in a drum which he forced him to fill with water. World Hope International staff came together with Ibrahim and pleaded also with the crowd. They said if the fellow who was amputated has forgiven him and is now pleading for him, it is wiser for the crowd to see reason to do the same and let him go. Reluctantly the people scattered but the fellow was kept inside for his own safety. As I was going home, people insulted me and referred to me as a fool who saw the man who amputated him and let him go free.

After the incident, the following day I went to see Sister Ann and explained to her all that transpired. She was happy with me for obeying God's word on forgiveness and encouraged me not to listen to what others will say.

The following Saturday I went back to Bible school and explained to Rev Donald Bestman who also was happy with me. He said that my action was not by myself but by divine inspiration and help.

I continued school, but it came to a time when I could no longer afford to pay my fees and even transport to go to school. One day I had made up my mind not to go to school because of lack of transportation, so Mrs. Conteh, who was the manager of the Javouhey House saw me and asked why I didn't go to school. I explained why and she helped me with transport and lunch that enabled me to go to school that day. She further encouraged me to continue.

That day at school the Director's mother, Mammy Gander, asked me how I was coping in school since Bill was no longer around to help me. I told her that it was out of my vegetable sales that I managed to keep attending. She promised that day to start paying my fees and I expressed gratitude. My only challenge was transport, lunch and materials. I had already made up my mind to stop the school after second year graduation, when one day at the Javouhey House as I passed by, a man named Joe Bacher called me and told me that the Lord would use me and afterward called Mark Stewart and he also said that God loves me and will surely use me for His glory. They brought anointing oil and anointed and prayed for me. Afterwards they gave me two books, <u>The Power of Forgiveness</u> and <u>A Cup of Living Water for a Hurting Soul</u> and after that, they hugged me which made me feel very good. They told Samuel Menyongar about me and he said that I used to go to Bible School through the support of Bill at IMC, but he did not know if I were still in school because Bill was no longer there. Then they asked me how I had been taking care of my schooling and I explained and they promised to start paying for me. After that they asked which department I was in at the Bible School and I told them that I was in the Evangelism Department. They told me that is exactly what they were involved in and invited me to join them the following day to see what they were doing. I was with them for a week, involved in their evangelism outreach in Aberdeen and Grafton.

Before they left, they handed me to Pastor Samuel Menyongar, Pastor Felix and Pastor Isaac and told them that I was now part of Hope Universal. This is how I started working with Hope Universal. My initial stipend was Le 15,000 which I highly appreciated. I still continued school while working with Hope.

I reached the end of my third and final year at the Bible School. I had paid for the graduation fees but still had to buy a neck tie, sash, trousers, gown, miter and other graduation materials. While I sat in class one morning contemplating on how I would handle this issue, I received a call from Administration. Initially I thought I was called to be asked out of the graduation ceremony because of the outstanding material needed for the graduation. On my arrival I was given a receipt of payment for all I needed for the ceremony by one Pastor Issa Turay of Faith Assemblies of God, Brookfields. I was so excited that I returned to class in a state joy and overwhelming gladness, hitting and banging everything that stood in my way.

The graduation came and I still had some problems. I was unable to get a gown so I borrowed one from a former student of the school. The gown was in such a bad condition but I had no alternative. As we stood in the line in readiness for the march, the staff went around inspecting every student. When they got to me, they noticed the gown and asked me to leave the line. I left the line and started crying. As I cried, another member of the staff saw me and got concerned. He came and asked me why and I told him that they had asked me to leave the line because of the condition of my gown. The fellow went and called Brother "Dee," as we use to call the Director of the school, and they both came and, after discussion, asked me to join the line. I rejoined the line, though hesitant and a bit ashamed, and the procession moved on.

From Victoria Park we matched to the National Stadium and converged at the Presidential Lounge where the graduation was held. I had invited many people to witness my graduation ceremony but only Sister Ann came. The lounge was packed full with graduates and well-wishers who came to witness the graduation ceremony. It was a colorful event and to me remarkable as I was leaving the school after three years of rigorous study to the work of the ministry. My only gift during this graduation came from Aunty Margaret Tommy. She gave me a rubber bowl which I highly appreciated.

CHAPTER SEVEN

MUSLIMS AT MANGO

I was in Congo Town near Freetown, close to the sea-shore, as a Muslim, but when someone invited me to church, I would attend, so my neighbours started calling me a Crismus, meaning Christian Muslim. There is a particular mango tree, surrounded by stones, where we always met to pray as Muslims. We would sit on the large stones and tell stories from our past including the sufferings experienced during the war. Many young men had lost hands, arms and some had lost legs as the cruel rebels attacked our villages. We tried to explain what had happened to us, but there were no logical explanations to the actions and hatred we had seen.

One day during Muslim fast month of Ramadan, I was keeping the fast and I was invited by a sister to attend a church service at the Christian Life Era Church. I started praying to God to lead me the place where he wanted me to become either Muslim or Christian. I had never prayed like this before and really did not know how to pray. I was there until 11:00 p.m. and I got up and went home. I had felt a strong urge to respond to the gospel preached in that little church, but since I had been a Muslim all my life and had seen how the Muslim community rejected those who professed to become Christians, I was afraid to make that move.

After ending the fast, I went to the next corner where they were selling different types of hard wine and marijuana under a large mango tree. Gamblers always met there and it was known as Confusion Corner. I started going there and people who came there to buy food would give part of their food to me. They told me that if I would smoke marijuana, I would forget all of my problems. I tried smoking but my problems didn't stop, I still had no hands and the smoke caused new problems. After smoking marijuana, I would fall asleep and sleep for a long time. After waking up from sleep, I would feel hungry and I didn't have any money to buy food. It made me feel very week and lazy and it added many more problems to my old problems. After smoking for many months, I finally stopped smoking but I was regularly there to collect leftover food. Later, the owner of the business asked me to be his assistant in selling the marijuana, saying that when the police came they would not arrest me because my two hands were cut off. Later, the owner of the business became very sick and he decided to go to another place with all his business.

After becoming a Christian, I usually went up to Leicester Peak on a retreat each year, sometimes two times a year. In 2005 I meet a lady who was very attractive to me and seemed to be interested in me. We believed that we were in love and thought we could begin our own family. When we met with her parents, my life was totally upset as her father said,

"Bambay, you cannot provide for our daughter, you can't even provide for yourself without hands."

At that time, I thought my life was over and I became discouraged; sometimes I would lock myself inside the room for the whole day and not eat food but kept crying. Once again, the thoughts of suicide that I had experienced at the hospital returned.

It happened about one week later, when I decided to stroll to Leicester Peak and sit under a mango tree close to the entrance of the Javouhey House. There I started to pray under the mango tree. That mango tree became my deliverance place, as I spent three days there praying to God that, if she were not the one, that God would show me the true one to be my real wife, one who could accept me as I am without hands.

CHAPTER EIGHT

FOOTBALL BLESSINGS

As I grew in the Lord and in the work of the ministry, God began to give me a vision. In my dreams I always had seen myself on the football field with a megaphone, preaching the gospel to the spectators and players. This continued over and over again for a long time. I even shared it with my colleague pastors and they said that it might be that the Lord wanted me to have a ministry of the gospel to footballers. As time went on, it became clear that He actually did want me to set up a football gospel ministry. This was how I founded the ministry now known as FC Seattle. This football club was primarily set up to reach out with the gospel of Jesus to the unreached.

Initially, we started it without a name until later when some missionaries visited with Hope Universal Sierra Leone and a couple among the visiting missionaries came to learn that we had a gospel football club. Eric and Becky Baker were so excited to know about the club and asked what the present pressing needs were. We shared with them and immediately they provided some help. They asked me the name of the club, and I told them we didn't have a name yet. Later, they advised that we consider the name FC Seattle and after careful consideration we adopted the name and it became the official name of our gospel football club.

The Lord also gave me visions of a church ministry which was meant to provide spiritual home to the many souls that were being saved through our outreach ministry. Situated in upper George Brook, back of the U.S Embassy (Kamara compound) within the IMATT area, is a community based church that has grown rapidly over several years with a congregation of about 250 members. The late Mr. Ibrahim Sorry Kamara and Joseph B. Kamara, his son, together with his family offered a place for the church. We began meeting there and they even rented a house adjoining the church where our family could live. They were very good to my family and excited about the new church in their community. I came to know this Kamara family through my friend Joseph B. Kamara who was very much involved in football and strong follower of Jesus Christ.

We called this new church God's Family Fellowship Church and decided that we would be independent of major church organizations and would simply worship God as His family. Initially a few people came other than the Kamaras and my family, but then the Lord started sending folks from the community around the US Embassy. We began to grow and see folks coming to trust Jesus as Savior. Soon some of the Muslim men were offended that their wives were meeting with us, so they refused to allow them to come. They would allow their children to come due to our soccer program, and over time we developed a good relationship, more through soccer than the gospel, but we thanked God for the door that He allowed to open through soccer. In Sierra Leone soccer is almost a religion that supersedes other religions, including Islam. The church continued to grow and continues today under the leadership of Joseph Kamara.

From the year 1998 to 1999, while I was with Sister Ann at the St Joseph Convent in Makeni, I was greatly discouraged because both my hands were cut off, but thank God for Sister Ann who tried to encourage me and later knowing that we loved football so much, she bought a football for us to play at the back of the Convent compound. I used to go there every morning and evening to play football and sometimes I would be there all day enjoying the games. Beside the field there was a local cookery shop and I use to go there to eat food. The owner of the local cookery shop had an adopted daughter by the name of Mary Kaloku, who helped her at the shop. She normally used to help feed me at their cookery shop since at that time I was not able to feed myself because of the pain that I was going through. Mary Kaloku normally came close to me and encouraged me. Mary was not afraid to come close to me, even though I had no hands. One day I visited her at their home around 3:30 p.m. and we had some time together. I told her that I was going to the soccer field and she asked if she could go with me. As we were going, I asked her why she was not afraid to come close to me as some people were.

Mary said, "I come close to you because I have always admired at you."

The next day Makeni was attacked by the R.U.F. rebels and we scattered.

It was not until 2002 when I got back to Makeni and went to the same cookery shop to eat rice, that I met this same lady at the shop, but I did not recognize her. I asked her for food but she said there was no food at all, but she was looking at me and I was afraid to look at her, so I started to ask her about a lady I had met there quite a long time ago. Immediately after I asked the question, she smiled and I recognized her as Mary, who had served me some years earlier, so I spent some time there as we renewed our memories of the past.

I was living with my friend, Mr. Ibrahim, and I told him that I loved Mary as my future wife.

But he asked me, "Have you ever talked to her?"

I replied, "No sir. But I want to go back and talk to her about my feelings"

Mr. Ibrahim replied, "Yes, go back and talk to her."

I was afraid, so I started to Mary's house, but then returned home before reaching her home. After three days I went there and I was not able to talk to her but she told me that she would talk to me later. Some days later I met with her again and this time she was able to talk to me, but she gave no answer regarding her feelings for me. After one month she gave me the answer,

Mary said, "OK, I do have special feelings for you, but I believe I should finish my education before we become serious."

I promised her that I was happy about that. As she continued with her plans, one night I received a phone call at 3:15 a.m. and she told me that she was in Freetown at her sister's house and we discussed her school.

Mary said, "I have not been able to continue school due to the lack of financial support."

Then she asked me to visit her one day. I decided to visit her, but as soon as I arrived at their home, her elder sister received me straight to the parlor where we spent time, but I was not able to talk to Mary because her sister thought that I had come there to visit her alone, so she gave no chance for me to see Mary. This happened three times, so I decided to take it to the Lord in prayer.

I prayed, "Dear Lord, please prevent the sister from interrupting my time with Mary."

The next time, my prayers were answered and I was allowed to spend time with Mary. When we met, I told Mary that I loved her and wanted her to be my wife. I really did not know how she would respond, but thankfully she expressed her love for me and I was so happy. At that point we agreed to be married and start a Christian home.

Our wedding was March 31, 2008, in Makeni and we started our married life in Freetown and later we moved to Konde Farm to serve with Pastor Samuel Menyongar. After a few months at Konde Farm, thieves broke into our home and stole most of our property. Mary reported the loss to her Uncle Marin who advised us to leave this place and either rent another place or return to Makeni. I told Sister Ann Stevens and she provided transportation to move us to the Javouhey House where we received housing and food during the transition.

I continued to work with the growth of FC Seattle, with the blessing of God working through Eric and Becky Baker who visited each year and communicated to supporters in the USA all year. Together we decided to expand the soccer ministry to Makeni, where Mary and I had family and had been given a house in the Amputee Village that was not being used. Soon we had teams in Freetown and Makeni and many young people were hearing the gospel of Jesus Christ and trusting Him.

CHAPTER NINE

RETURN TO THE BEGINNING

F ollowing the peace treaty and the news of the terrible wounds suffered by the people of Sierra Leone, many people from all over the world wanted to help with the recovery process. One such group was from Denmark, and they decided to develop an amputee village near Makeni where they built nice houses and offered them to amputees at no charge. This seemed like a great opportunity in one way but a possible stumbling block in other ways. I was now working with Hope Universal and had the benefit of accountability and fellowship with other Christian workers at Hope. In 2015, during the Ebola outbreak, Mary and I moved from Freetown to Makeni to expand the FC Seattle soccer ministry and to begin an orphanage for children who had lost parents to Ebola. In July, 2016, we started a church under the mango trees near our new chicken house and garden where we are presently worshiping.

I started this story at Mahawa with the planting of my first mango tree. I am now married to Mary and we have three children and twenty-five orphans, and we are back in Makeni and thanking our Lord Jesus every day for the amazing grace He has shown a poor farmer with no hands. We started with one mango tree and now we have the blessing of meeting under a grove of mango trees each week.

The first mango tree provided shade and good fruit, plus a community meeting place for friends and family. Our mango grove provides a place for the "fruit of the Spirit" to be demonstrated as we meet to worship and plan programs to reach our community with the gospel of Jesus Christ. Part of that long-range plan is to build a church at Mahawa where my hands are buried along with the hands of many former family members and friends. The land has been purchased and many folks are praying and giving time and money to complete this project. It reminds me of the quote by Joseph in Genesis 50:20:

"But as for you, you meant evil against me, but God meant it for good, in order to bring about as it is this day, to save many people alive."

The Lord has also blessed me with Mary to remove the depression of the past and three great children to challenge our faith for the future. As we work together with children of our own, plus many orphans, we claim the scripture verse on the entrance to the orphanage which says if we "train up a child in the way he should go, when he is old he will not depart from it."Proverbs 22:6

CHAPTER TEN

GREAT LESSONS LEARNED

S ome of you who read this book may be discouraged due to your family history, mistakes you have made, sickness and various handicaps, or other difficult issues of life. As I have struggled with the loss of both hands, thoughts of suicide, and fears of failure, the Lord has spoken to me through other Christians and revealed through His word His great power available to a poor farmer with no hands, using verses like Ephesians 3:20: "My God is able to do exceedingly abundantly above all we ask or think, according to the power that works in us."

My first great lesson is that my God has unlimited power that He is willing and ready to put to work in my weakness to do great things.

Some of you may be discouraged because to date you have been unable to find the mate that God has planned for you. As you have seen in my experience,

71

sometimes our first impression of the right one may not be God's best for us. When we submit to God's will, He will direct us to the right mate. I thank God for Mary and I know she is God's best for me.

> **My second great lesson is that my God loves to direct us to the mate through whom He can produce a picture of the relationship of Christ and the church.**

Some of you may be struggling financially as you provide for your family and others in need. God has not promised to give us what we want, but He has promised to meet all our needs based on His ability to pay, which is unlimited. We read in Philippians 4:19, "My God shall supply all your need according to His riches in glory by Christ Jesus."

> **My third great lesson is that my God knows what I need and He never runs out of funds to meet those needs.**

CPSIA information can be obtained
at www.ICGtesting.com
Printed in the USA
FFOW03n1730270218
45321977-45990FF